JUST
CONFIRMED

YOUR LIFE AHEAD
AS A YOUNG CATHOLIC

SUSAN SAYERS

Kevin
Mayhew

First published in 1997 by
KEVIN MAYHEW LTD
Buxhall, Stowmarket, Suffolk IP14 3BW
Email: info@kevinmayhewltd.com

9 8 7 6 5 4 3 2 1

ISBN 1 84003 108 5
Catalogue No 1500157

Edited by David Gatward and Robert Kelly
Cover design by Jonathan Stroulger
Cartoons by Fred Chevalier
Typesetting by Louise Selfe

Printed and bound in Great Britain

Contents

For Sam, Luke, Mark, Luke, Elisabeth, Laura, Gracie, Abigail, Alex and Jane whom I had in mind while this book was being written, and for all future 'Living Stones' as they are confirmed.

'I have set before you life and death. Now choose life, so that you and your children may live and that you may love the Lord your God, listen to his voice and hold fast to him.'

Deuteronomy 30:19, 20

INTRODUCTION

Welcome! You might well be wondering why you have been given this book. After all, you've just completed a course preparing you for the sacrament of confirmation, and the bishop has anointed you with chrism and confirmed you. So that's it, isn't it?

Lots of us see confirmation as the finishing line. At last you're an adult Christian, committing yourself to Jesus for life. It is very like coming of age, only you may not yet be able to vote or get married or buy alcohol. It seems to mark the end of your childhood in the church, and it can feel as if you've suddenly been pushed out into open water to sink or swim.

But it's not really a finishing at all. More a case of reaching the starting line in a way. Perhaps you were baptised when you were a baby and have been brought up in a family where some or all of your close relatives are used to praying and going to church regularly. In which case you've probably got to know God very well over the years, almost without realising it.

Or perhaps you've only recently started coming to church, and a lot of things seem strange still, but you know enough about God to sense that you can trust him with anything.

Well, wherever you are coming from, you've reached the starting line, and have the rest of your life ahead of you to spend in company with God, who loves you. This book is a kind of travel guide to help you on your journey. It's got the equivalent of spiritual maps and charts to help you plan and keep to the route, survival techniques for when the going gets rough, emergency help and a highway code.

Some of this book you write yourself – I've left spaces for your bits – so that it will become a very personal handbook and a handy reference manual which you can add to over the next few years.

Read it straight through, and then dip into it regularly, keeping it near your Bible. You don't have to pretend you're some sort of holy person to use this handbook – it isn't written for super gurus, so being yourself is just fine.

ABOUT GOD

God believes in you. He doesn't wonder if you exist, he knows you do, because he was there at the beginning of you, and watched you growing from a clump of cells into the thinking, moving, feeling specimen you are now. And he didn't keep looking at you and wishing you had different hair, or different shaped feet, or different (or more) talents, because he likes the way you are and wouldn't want you any different.

He isn't always delighted by the way you behave, of course, especially when you make things difficult and painful for yourself or other people, but even then he understands why you do the things you do and is ready to help you sort things out if they've gone wrong. To God you are known personally – by your name – and when Jesus says 'Know I am with you always' (Matthew 28:20), it isn't some vague generalisation but a solemn promise.

When Jesus says, 'Know I am with you always', he means that

is going to have the personal company of Jesus, Son of God, for their entire life, and whenever

speaks to God or asks him about something, God will already know all the circumstances and be listening, because

is his own loved child and close friend.

PROMISES AND QUESTIONS

PROMISES, PROMISES

At your confirmation you made some promises which reaffirmed what was promised (either by you, or for you if you were too young) at your baptism. This is what you said:

'I turn to Christ,
I repent of my sins.'

God has believed in you all along, and always will. Now you were prepared to stand up in public and say 'Yes, I know God is real. I

13

know he's alive and that he loves us all. And I intend to live my life aware of him, rather than ignoring him, or only keeping in touch with him when I feel like it. I'd like this to be teamwork; God and me in partnership.'

For his part, God has promised to give you everything you need for this partnership. All his power, all his grace, is freely available to you all the time you live in his company, and wherever you end up, all through your life, you'll have access to all you need to cope with any situation whatsoever.

That doesn't mean that God has a Santa's grotto full of goodies and will dish out bikes and marriage partners and exam answers whenever we want. God's idea of what we need may seem a bit obscure or even downright awkward at times. That's because he's interested in our eternal life, as well as this section we live on earth, and it might be more necessary for us to acquire patience, for instance, rather than always having what we want straight away. And it might sometimes be more necessary for us to be available to baby-sit, for instance, than to be out every night with our friends. God isn't planning to turn us into spoilt brats.

But although it takes time to get used to seeing the good in some of God's ideas, eventually – often when we look back – we can see how God has used some awful or tragic event and brought good out of it. That's the way God always works. He's not some grinning power maniac who enjoys making life difficult for people 'because it's good for them'. What he does is grieve over all those terrible things that happen and turn them upside down to transform them.

Like the stories you've probably heard of the way people in the blitz made deep friendships and looked after one another, during that destructive time of war when homes would be bombed and wiped out overnight and loved ones left and never came back. Having chosen to give us the very dangerous gift of free will, God knows that he will often be sharing in the deep pain caused by evil, but he keeps his promise to use even that evil for some good.

QUESTIONS, QUESTIONS

It's not only wartime that has tragedy, of course. Perhaps you have sometimes seen the news and wondered how there can possibly be a loving God if all this evil and violence is going on. If God loves us so much, why doesn't he do something to stop it? (If this is something you worry about a lot, go to page 86 and read that.)

Another thing that puzzles lots of us about

God is: Who made him? How did he start? It's all very well to say, 'Oh, that's easy, no one made God. God's always been there.' (Which is true.) But it's so hard when our human brains start trying to understand something so seemingly freaky as not having a beginning and an end. (This whole puzzle is explored on page 84.)

So while we believe that God really exists, and loves us, there are heaps of questions that will keep popping up about him as we go through life. *Never feel that these questions which come into your mind are wrong!* Never feel they are evidence that you're not a real Christian after all and that you might as well stop 'pretending'. Lots of people stop praying, stop reading the Bible and stop going to church when they find themselves asking questions.

That is a great pity because questions like these are actually the sign of good progress! They show that your spiritual life is growing, honestly, frankly and effectively. (Do you remember what Jesus' parents found him doing when they had lost him in Jerusalem? He was asking questions.) Through your questions God will be able to help you get to know deep truths about himself and the universe, about other people, and even about yourself which you couldn't have understood before.

So the last thing you need to do is opt out of his company, just as things are taking off. When the questions come (and they will) keep on with your praying and your reading of scripture, listening out for God's answers. (More about how God answers on page 27.) God will not let you down, and he is quite unshockable, so whatever the questions are, you can tell him what's on your mind.

MY QUESTIONS

Now it's your turn to write a bit of this book. In the space at the end of this section write down any questions about God (and life) which puzzle you. Hopefully, you won't fill it all straight away! You may have some already which keep coming back to you over and over again. This space is here for you to jot down all the questions as they happen, thrown up by things which happen to you (or don't happen) and by things you've seen or heard or read about. Jot the questions down straight away; if you're anything like me you'll forget if you leave it a while.

You are probably wondering what point there is in writing your questions down. Well, firstly, writing them down in this book will remind you that the questions are a healthy part of the journey. Secondly, recording them will help you remember them and enable you and God together to deal with them properly, in due time, instead of chucking them out. Thirdly, as you journey through life you will be able to look back over your past questions and tell yourself the answers that God has shown you. So they will be a way of keeping a record of your journey – a bit like a photo album of yourself.

Date	Why? What? How? When?

Date	Why? What? How? When?

<u>Keeping in Touch</u>

Praying used to be the ordinary word for asking. You might have said, 'I pray you, pass the peanut butter.' Or, 'Why are we missing every goal in this match, I pray?'

We can easily think that praying to God is asking him for things, so that prayer is rather like those lists you get given before a group holiday to remind you what to pack. Then you can go through the list of people and situations to ask God to help, and put it away again until next time.

In fact, only a part of praying is asking, and

what praying really means is keeping in touch with God. You don't keep in touch with your friends and your family by asking them for things all the time. Imagine it! They'd think you'd lost it completely.

When you think of prayer as keeping in touch with God you can see that:

- it needn't always involve words (For example, showing your love for someone by doing something kind or caring? What about watching or listening to something together without saying much apart from the odd comment?)
- it can be pouring out your story, your anger, your excitement, your indignation or your misery
- it can be thinking of the other person and what they would like
- it can be listening to what they have to say
- it can be a quick hug or a purposeful glance across the room, while you're busy
- it can be telling them how you feel about them
- it can be saying sorry and knowing they forgive you
- it can be enjoying things they have made for you and thanking them

Praying is all these things. It's also a very natural thing which you can do in your own natural words. You don't need any lessons in grammar or Gothic because God knows you really well already.

Perhaps you're the kind of person who neatly lays out everything on the bed before you pack a rucksack. Or perhaps you're more likely to grab handfuls of clothes in any order and stuff them in all together. You will probably find that your praying will reflect the way you do other things, and God will still know you're in touch, however you do it. He'll take what you are naturally and build on that. We have to keep remembering that God doesn't have our human limitations, and can cope with all our different ways.

More than anything, he longs for us to keep in touch and so he's happy for us to speak in our usual way, using the kind of words we feel comfortable with. Sometimes you will come across a prayer written by someone else which exactly expresses what you wanted to say. It may have been born out of years of living closely in God's company. In which case, use it. Lovers will sometimes give one another poems for the same reason. Greetings cards include messages which the senders can adopt as their own.

But for the most part, we need to get used to keeping in touch with God in our own language and character, and give translators and interpreters some time off.

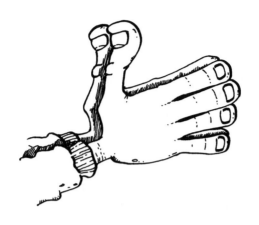

PRAYER

WHERE SHOULD I PRAY?

You can pray anywhere. God is not tied down to any one place, so you can pray in shops, on the bus, in the corridors, in the bathroom, having your hair cut, at the disco, in bed or on holiday.

You do need a regular time every day to do nothing but pray, and for practical reasons this needs to be somewhere you can be alone, or at least left alone. Lots of people find this space in bed at the beginning and end of the day, and this is fine except that you can easily nod off. Some people find that walking the dog is a good time, or on a paper round.

Think around the times in your day which leave you able to concentrate and if you haven't got such a time, make one by setting the alarm earlier. (If you are planning to do this, don't forget to stagger off to bed a bit earlier as well.)

Having decided on a time, write it in the space below so that it becomes a commitment. Then you're more likely to keep to it until it becomes a good habit. Once this has happened you'll find that you miss it badly if for any reason you aren't able to keep the appointment. Because that's what it is – an important appointment with the One who made you and loves you.

> My Prayer Time:

How do I start?

If you have an appointment to keep with one of your mates you have to go to the meeting place and look out for them until you recognise them. Then you greet them in some way – passionate embrace, slurpy snog, slap on the back, nervous smile, depending on the company and how well you know them. Or maybe just a friendly 'hello'. With God, too, you need to settle down and look out for him rather than launching straight into some prayers.

That's why the important parts of the liturgy often start in this way:

'The Lord be with you.'
'And also with you.'

Obvious, really, but we need to say it to remind ourselves of what we're doing and who we're meeting.

So take time to put down whatever you were doing (including sleeping) and think to yourself, 'I'm putting this time aside at the beginning/end of the day to get in touch with God . . . God is here. Now.'

Some people find it helps to concentrate on their breathing, because that focuses on being alive, and it also helps quieten you down and get you settled. As you breathe in you can think of yourself breathing in God's peace. As you breathe out, think of breathing out all your worry and your deadlines and everything that crowds your thinking. So in a while you've put things down and have reminded yourself of what is true all the time – God is alive and keeping in touch with you. (By the way, that's where the word 'inspiration' comes from – 'in-breathing'.)

HOW DOES GOD ANSWER PRAYER?

When you have a conversation with another human, you hear their voice replying to you through your ears, see their expression with your eyes and feel their gestures with your body. If someone sat expressionless and in complete silence and later told you they had been talking to you, you'd either assume you had gone completely deaf or that they were having you on.

So when Jesus assures us that God always answers our prayer, and yet we can't see his mouth moving or hear an actual voice, what are we to think? Is God having us on? Does he really answer us or are we kidding ourselves?

Well, he isn't pretending; the truth is that God actually does answer our prayers. He actually does speak to us and tell us things. But since he is God, he doesn't do it in the same way as just another human would, and if we are to hear his voice we need to tune in to it. Otherwise it's a bit like puzzling over why we can't tune in to our favourite TV sit-com when it's actually the hot wash programme on the washing machine we have switched on.

God doesn't have to speak to us through the ears because he has direct access to our thinking, our imagination, our heart and emotions. And he uses all these channels as appropriate. Suppose you have been talking to God about how to sort out your very complicated love life, or about needing a week-end job that will still leave you enough time to get your homework done. You may then find that out of the blue, when you're not thinking about anything in particular, an idea comes to you, or a different way of understanding, that will solve the problem. That idea was spoken into your mind by God.

Suppose you have been worrying about finances and have confided in God. Before the practical details are sorted out you may suddenly experience a sense that you know it's going to be all right, and you don't feel so worried. There's no way you can give people rigid proof that God has spoken peace of mind into you, but you simply know; God has given you his reassurance in secret.

Suppose you have to sort out a misunderstanding with someone, and ask for God's help beforehand. When you arrive, you sense that the person is reacting more warmly, or is able to cope with what you are saying better than you expected. God has been speaking into the fears of both of you and allowing you both to get things sorted out well.

It's impressive, isn't it? And this service is completely freely available to everyone. You just happen to be one of those who are using it. Imagine what could happen in our society if more of us were tuned in!

So God speaks directly into our thoughts, feelings and needs. He speaks in other ways as well. He speaks through events and things you see and read. What he does is to use events and sights you would be noticing anyway, and draw your spiritual attention to them so that they help you understand something. Perhaps you have been asking God to show you if a particular career choice is right for you, so you can choose your options accordingly. Later on you are buying a CD and are told the one you wanted is no longer available. The one they offer instead turns out to be even better.

Suddenly your prayer springs into your mind and you know that God is guiding you to see this ordinary event as an illustration: the career God has in mind may not be what you have in mind at the moment but will turn out to be even better for you. Now your prayer will be to find out what this is. You and God are having an ongoing conversation, and he is talking to you in stories, or parables.

Of course, you don't have to go around with a spiritual magnifying glass, peering into every event to see if it has deep significance! But you do need to know that God can speak this way, so that you're prepared to notice when it happens. And it will be quite obvious, because the significance will occur to you suddenly and clearly.

Another way God speaks is through conversations you have with other people. Again, you may be thinking over what you talked about and suddenly realise that it has helped you understand something you were praying about. God has used the conversation and spoken to you through it. He is also likely to use you sometimes to answer other people's prayers, which is quite a thought.

Suppose I miss important things out?

When Jesus' disciples asked him to teach them to pray he gave them an excellent pattern or model to use. We know it as 'The Lord's Prayer'. It helps us get our priorities right and makes sure we don't leave out anything important. And since Jesus suggested it, it seems a good idea to use it. But Jesus meant it as a pattern, not a ready-made prayer to be churned out. If we are to use it as a model, as Jesus intended, then we need to take each phrase and use it as a heading, like this:

Our Father who art in heaven

In a way you've already been doing this heading as you made a deliberate choice to spend time in God's company. Once you are still, enjoy being a child in God's family. That makes God your loving parent. The actual word Jesus used was 'Abba', which is like saying 'Daddy'. If the notion of 'father' picks up on images you find painful, think instead of the mothering love of God, or the love of a grandparent, if that is where you have learnt about faithful caring and total acceptance. And if all family titles disturb you and are linked in your mind with rejection instead of acceptance, go for the word 'God' and know that what Jesus was getting at was the kind of loving parenting you'd love to have known and never have. God is the kind of parent you yourself would most like to be for your own children. That is the kind of parenting this God can give you for the whole of your life. And this God is giving you his full attention right now.

Hallowed be your name

'Hallowed' is a bit like the word 'haloed'. Like that hazy glow around the moon some nights in winter, or the softened filtered light effect some smart cameras can give you, so you can create rather mystical beauty in your photographs. Holding God's name holy, or hallowed, is like a lifting of your heart in sensing the wonder and beauty and mystery of all that 'God' means.

The thinker and creator of all the richness in our universe is lovingly attentive to you. You can actually communicate with the One who made you and gave you life.

You may not need words. If we see something incredibly wonderful – a wide view when the fog lifts on a mountain; a creature being born; a spectacular fireworks display – we're often reduced to an intake of breath, oohs, ahs and wows. This is the 'wow' part of your prayer, when your heart is excited and awed by who God is and your worship of him.

May your kingdom come;
may your will be done on earth
as it is in heaven

This is the 'work' part of prayer. All of us who pray for God's kingdom to come and God's will to be done are helping to fling open the battened-down hatches of our world to let in the air and sunlight of God's love. So what kind of kingdom are we wanting to be established and to grow? And why do we want it?

We can get a mistaken idea of God as king if we link it to our experience of a figurehead with little real power or a powerful leader who insists on his own way, whatever the ordinary people might want. God's kingdom is not like either of these images. God's kingdom concerns the spirit or the soul and is all about goodness, right living, love, joy, peace of mind and wise understanding. It is about real justice, sensitivity to people's needs and hurts, mutual respect and mutual reverence.

So in this section of prayer we long for God to heal and mend what is broken in people's lives, for unjust laws and social practices to be changed; for lives imprisoned by guilt or evil or fear to be set free. We long for God to be let in to the lives of our friends, neighbours, families and work mates.

Again, you may not want to use words. Pictures of people and situations may form in your mind which you think about, with that longing for God's transforming love in your heart. Or you may simply name particular people and situations, bringing them to mind in God's presence. It may help to think of each person in a room with windows, and as you name them before God, imagine yourself opening the curtains, opening the windows, and inviting God's sunlight in.

You may have particular needs for people which you can tell God about. He knows already, of course, but he also knows it helps you to express it, and it opens the way for him to work as you ask for his kingdom to come in this particular area of their lives.

Give us this day our daily bread

When the people of Israel were in the desert, they only gathered enough manna for a day at a time (see Exodus, chapter 16). And Jesus taught us not to fill our minds with lots of long-term worries (see Matthew's gospel, chapter 6, verses 25 and following). Each day, he said, has quite enough for us to worry about.

You might feel that since you have a supermarket down the road and a spare loaf in the freezer you don't need to pray for daily bread.

What this heading does is remind us that we actually rely on God for everything, so in asking our God for the basic needs we are saying, 'I know we depend on you for life and survival'. Notice, too, that Jesus expects us to say 'our'. It isn't just for myself that I pray, but we pray for all people. And we can hardly ask God to provide daily needs for people who end up starving because we fail to speak out against exploitation. So, very cunningly, God gets us responsibly involved in the feeding. Or rather, the just sharing as there is enough for all if we are not greedy. This section can apply to lots of basic needs, and not only physical bread. Any needs – spiritual, physical, mental, emotional or social can be brought to mind here either in words or pictures in our mind's eye.

And forgive us our trespasses
as we forgive those who trespass against us

Coming straight after the 'give us' section, 'for-give' is like asking God to take back, or take away from us the sin, the mean thinking, the selfish behaviour, the cruel gossip, the cheating and lies, the greed and sexually sordid – all that we know is not what God has called us into, but that we have done and been anyway. Only God can forgive, or take away sin. But he's an expert at it and when he takes our sin away, it isn't there in us any more, and we are completely free to start again.

And lead us not into temptation
But deliver us from evil

Left to ourselves we blunder straight into temptations until they are so strong we give up trying to resist them. It's rather like the difference between choosing a firm or badly eroded path. The more treacherous the path we choose, the more likely we are to trip and hurt ourselves.

God offers himself as a free mountain guide, used to the terrain and conditions ahead. If we accept his offer, and ask him to lead us, he will pick the best route for us through circumstances and temptations to prevent us falling. And, when we have got ourselves snarled up in evil, our guiding God will rescue us, and set us free again.

PRAYER PATTERNS

Our Father who art in heaven . . .

Stop. Think what this means.

. . . hallowed be your name

Think of places in the world and in your life where it isn't hallowed.

May your kingdom come.

Long for this.
Put down your own kingdom for a minute and long for God's.

May your will be done
on earth as it is in heaven.

> *Think over particular situations where you*
> *want God's will to be done.*

Give us this day our daily bread.

> *Talk over with God any particular needs*
> *and problems you and the world face*
> *today and ask for his help.*
> *Ask God to show you how you can help*
> *'feed' others through the day.*

Forgive us our trespasses
as we forgive those
who trespass against us.

> *Be brave, be honest.*
> *Face up to what your sins are.*
> *Never forget that you can be forgiven and*
> *you will feel much better when you're free.*
> *This is the bargain section; you have to*
> *forgive those who have wronged you.*
> *Do it now.*

Lead us not into temptation,
but deliver us from evil

> *Invite God into the whole day.*
> *Check any relationships or activities where*
> *God is advising you not to go.*
> *Listen to his advice.*

Amen.

HELPFUL PRAYERS

Here are some prayers of other Christians
through history which you may well find
useful:

> Holy God, holy and strong
> holy and immortal,
> have mercy on us.
> Holy God, holy and strong,
> holy and immortal,
> I worship you!

> My Lord and my God!

> God . . . is . . . now . . .

Hide me under the shadow of your wings.

> Save us, O Lord, while we are awake;
> protect us while we are asleep;
> that we may keep watch with Christ
> and rest with him in peace.

> The Lord is my shepherd
> therefore I can never lack for anything.

> Almighty God
> to whom all hearts are open
> all desires known
> and from whom no secrets are hidden;

cleanse the thoughts of our hearts
by the inspiration of your Holy Spirit,
that we may perfectly love you
and worthily magnify
your holy name,
through Christ our Lord.

Deep peace of the running wave to you.
Deep peace of the flowing air to you.
Deep peace of the quiet earth to you.
Deep peace of the shining stars to you.
Deep peace of the Son of Peace to you.

God be in my head
and in my understanding,
God be in my eyes and in my looking.
God be in my mind and in my thinking.
God be at my end
and at my departing.

Lord make me an instrument of your peace;
where there is hatred, let me sow love;
where there is injury, pardon;
where there is despair, hope;
and where there is sadness, joy.
Divine Master, grant that I may seek
not so much to be consoled
as to console,
to be understood as to understand,
to be loved as to love.

For it is in giving that we receive,
it is in pardoning
that we are pardoned,
and in dying
that we are born to eternal life.

Thanks be to you,
my Lord Jesus Christ
for all the benefits which you have given me.
For all the pains and insults
you have borne for me.
O most merciful Redeemer,
Friend and Brother,
may I know you more clearly,
love you more dearly
and follow you more nearly, day by day.

Glory be to the Father
and to the Son
and to the Holy Spirit,
as it was in the beginning, is now
and shall be for ever.

Christ, as a light
illumine and guide us.
Christ, as a shield,
overshadow and cover us.
Christ be under us,
Christ be over us.
Christ be beside us

on left and on right.
Christ be before us,
Christ be behind us.
Christ be within us,
Christ be without us.
Christ, as a light,
illumine and guide us.

Save me, Lord, I am sinking!

Grant me the serenity
to accept the things I cannot change,
courage to change the things I can,
and wisdom to know the difference.

Yet I will rejoice in the Lord.

Bless this food to our use
and ourselves in your service
through Jesus Christ our Lord.

PRAYERS YOU FIND AND
WANT TO REMEMBER

PRAYING YOUR WAY THROUGH THE DAY

This section is to do with training yourself to remember that God is with you as often as your body is, because your body is part of where God lives. God's Holy Spirit has moved in, and every time you receive communion at the eucharist you are becoming more and more bound up together and part of one another. This isn't some kind of sinister take-over bid, where your own personality will gradually shrivel up and drop off. God does things differently. The more part of your life he becomes, the more your real self you will be. So if you want to reach your full potential as a person, the best way to do it is to keep referring to God, thanking him, thinking things over with him and listening out for him throughout the day.

How do you do this? It helps to label particular places or times of day where you decide to 'touch base'. (You might choose food, taps, mirrors, toilets and traffic lights, for instance.) Then you will find that whenever you come across these places they will act as reminders – ah, that's right, I remember – hello God! Then you can catch up on any thanking, thinking over, unburdening or questioning that needs to be done.

Another way to keep in contact with God is by having in your head various words from scripture or from songs which will come to mind when you aren't thinking of anything in particular. These may be songs you sang as a child, bits from hymns you sing at church, tracks from recordings of religious songs, and verses from the Bible which you have learnt by heart. Sometimes you will even find God using these to speak to you (more about that on page 56).

I was going to say that gradually you'll find you are keeping in touch with God regularly in between your memory joggers, but I know that for me it isn't quite like that. There are some days when you are really aware of walking through life very close to God, but there'll be other days when you are so busy that it's only at the memory joggers that you make conscious contact.

But it is possible to keep in touch with God however busy we get. And we don't need Einstein's brain to do it either. Suppose for a minute you've got to give a rather scary teacher an excuse about some homework you haven't done. And you're dreading it. Then your friend says they'll come along with you to keep you company. Even though the friend might not be saying anything, the meeting goes better because you are conscious of your friend standing there with you, by your side.

God is there in all those meetings and difficult conversations in a very similar way, and if we train ourselves to be conscious of his presence at our side it will really help us in what we say and how we react to others. God is never there as a spy. God is always there as a friend.

OTHER WAYS TO PRAY

PRAYER WALKING

A good idea which comes from the early Celtic Christians is soaking a place in prayer, rather as a gardener might soak the soil before planting cabbages in it. Those Celtic Christians wouldn't even think of starting to build a church without praying on the site for weeks or even months beforehand.

Suppose there is a particular area in the playground at school, or a particular street in your town where fights start, or drugs are available. Whenever you are near these places you can make a point of speaking to God and asking for the Holy Spirit to fill the area and touch the lives of those who come to it. You can pray round shops and in hospitals, on buses and in lifts in the same way. And you can pray the pews in church to prepare for the Sunday liturgy there.

Sometimes you may see immediate results. Someone may relax, or act kindly. A distressed child may stop crying. You may find yourself being used to help someone. An unexpected conversation may start up. Other times you may notice nothing, but you have prepared a little piece of ground, and God will use it in his good time. We once made a lasting friendship through leaving an advert for a garden shed in the local supermarket and praying over the advert for the people who would read it!

If you deliver papers you can pray God's blessing on each home and along each street, and know that you are giving people far more than just the paper they ordered. You may not ever see the results while you are in this life, but when you reach heaven you will find out just how God has used your prayers to be able to help those people.

Perhaps there are some people among your relatives or neighbours or classmates who really wind you up and get on your nerves. There's usually at least one at any one time in your life! No doubt you'll be talking this over with God anyway, but it can also help to prayer walk the place you have to be with them before you actually meet. This may mean praying the table as you lay it, praying the bus stop as you wait, or praying the park where you'll be playing.

PRAYING TOGETHER

So far we have only looked at ways to pray on your own. But as Christians we are called to be the body of Christ on earth, and when we talk about being 'members' of the church it means just that – bits of body. To dismember anything involves a lot of destruction, and stops it working. So it is important that as members of the body we meet together regularly to pray.

There may be communal prayer of one kind or another at your school (school assembly, class Masses, etc). If you don't like what is going on in school, pray about it, stick with it and allow God to transform anything which needs transforming. If you don't have class Masses, pray about it. Pray to meet others who share the same idea with you, but then be prepared to be used in the planning and preparation to make sure it happens.

Get together with a Christian friend (of any age) and commit yourselves to being prayer partners. This means that you promise to pray for each other each day, and whenever you need anything particular to be prayed for, you can contact your partner and they will pray as well. Sometimes you can pray together, other times on your own but at a prearranged time. You can support your friend in prayer when she or he is taking an important exam, for instance; or you can have prayer support while you are playing an important game.

PRAYING IN CHURCH

In liturgy, the whole Christian community can get together to praise the true God, learn more about him, and pray corporately (which means as a body). In the Catholic Church we can enjoy quite a wide range of traditions and styles of worship. Not only will you find variety from church to church, but also there are often different styles within the same church.

On a Sunday, for instance, there may be a quiet Mass early in the morning, and a family Mass mid-morning. Some places have special Masses for young people, not necessarily every week, but once a month or at least once a term. Some churches use mainly organ and choir to lead the singing, while others have a music group of different instruments, and many a mixture of both. In some liturgies and services you will find candlelight, colour, and fragrance from incense. Sometimes the music will be gentle, mystical melodies to help you set an atmosphere for meditative prayer; at others the music will be more lively, bursting with praise.

Some people find it easier to pray in public worship than on their own and some the other way round, and we need to work at both. Here are some ideas for making the most of the time you spend in church with your Christian family.

It really starts before you get to church at all. I've mentioned the possibility of walking round the church at some point during the week, praying along the pews, at the lectern and pulpit, altar and font. Think of the purpose of each part of the building, and let that become a prayer for those who will next use it. For example, at the font, pray for the next person that will be baptised there; dip your hand in the water and remember your own baptism, and pray for the strength and grace to live up to your baptismal promises.

When you wake up in the morning on Sunday and remember what day it is, tell God you are giving your worship time over to him, to use as he wants. After that you only need to be attentive. Perhaps you'll walk into church at the same time as someone who needs you to offer to sit with them and make them feel at home. Perhaps your skills – in the choir or music group, as a reader or as a server – will be needed to help others worship, so that your work is your prayer.

Perhaps God has something particular he wants you to grasp today, some answer to one of your questions, or some teaching that will really help you in the coming week. In which case you may find one particular verse of a hymn, or one of the readings, or something said in the sermon hits you hard, and suddenly makes important sense to you.

Lots of amazing and wonderful things can happen when the church gets together to pray, just as long as they are all there, and it isn't only their bodies sitting looking intelligent. Obviously your mind is bound to wander sometimes, but employ a sheep-dog to keep rounding up your wandering thoughts and bringing them back to what you have come for. If everyone in the congregation does this, and God has clear access to a whole churchful of people, he will really be able to work there and you will be able to feel the presence of God among you.

There are often books provided so that you

can follow the celebration. Do use these if they help you make the words and the rites your own. But don't forget that you can also use your ears and listen, using your eyes to look at flowers, stained glass, shadows or stonework, rather than words on a page.

The important thing is that the people gathered in church are not an audience, passively watching someone else's performance, but a congregation (which means a gathering together) where everyone present is involved in the work of worshipping God.

THE BIBLE

READING THE BIBLE

As you probably know, the Bible is not one book but a library of books under one cover. There are history books, letters, poetry, stories, biographies and songs. The writers are a very varied bunch, covering a wide stretch of time, and all writing for readers with different cultural backgrounds and interests. So the Bible is a fascinating collection of documents of immense value, whether you are a Christian or whether you are simply interested in the development of peoples and ideas.

Research is still going on, based on fragments of ancient scrolls, so that every year new light is shed on the Bible writings.

Archaeologists are increasingly able to make sense of things that have puzzled readers in the past. And readers in every generation find that in these scriptures there is help, reassurance, challenge, comfort and inspiration for their journey through life.

But how can such writings go on being relevant in each generation without getting out of date? Part of the answer is that they deal with the very deepest issues of what being human is all about, and since we're human, we all find we are asking the same questions – such as: Who am I? Where did we come from? Where will we go when we die? How should I live? Why do I end up doing evil when I want to do good?

There is a deep sense in which all the writings in the Bible 'live'. They come alive to people who read them, in widely different countries and in widely different ages. At first sight this may seem impossible, and yet it happens. How?

Christians talk about the Bible being inspired (or 'in-breathed') by God, and once God is in the equation, the whole picture changes, and what would usually be impossible, becomes quite normal. In some way God's spirit has been working in those Scriptures, right through from when the human writers first put pen to papyrus, to when you and I sit down to read chunks from our English versions today.

As a committed Christian it is important that you have regular access to this important book, so you will need to get hold of your own personal copy. Then you can write things in the margin, underline verses you find specially helpful, and jot down your own notes in the back, if you so wish.

Perhaps you have been given a copy of the Bible already. Nice as it is to be given a present, your Bible will not be very useful to you unless you can understand the language. So if you have been given a traditional Authorised Version by a fond, well-meaning relative, enjoy reading it from time to time for the poetry by all means. In fact, the Authorised Version is the translation which best respects the Greek of the Gospels and the New Testament letters, so it can be very handy for checking precise meanings. However, for everyday use, get yourself a good, reliable up-to-date version, suitable for your age group.

Here is a list of versions I would recommend:

• *The Children's Bible* (New Century version)
This book has good pictures, and the text is easy to read, with short sentences. In the back there are maps, a quiz, a Bible dictionary and space for notes. Although it's called a

children's Bible I know many adults who have found it useful.

• *The Youth Bible* (New Century version)

This has short Bible studies which are very relevant to real life situations, and interesting bits of information, and questions to challenge your thinking, which are scattered throughout the book. It's well translated with plenty of footnotes to help you in the difficult parts.

• *The Message* by Eugene Peterson

This is the whole of the New Testament; there is another book with Psalms and Proverbs from the Old Testament. It's very freely translated so that when you read it, it sounds just like talking.

• *The New International Version*

This is a version very widely used by Christians of all ages and denominations, because it is thoroughly researched and written in modern English. The study version of this Bible has excellent study notes, maps and concordance, so you can look up a keyword to find the verse you're looking for.

• *The Good News Bible*

This is another commonly used version with an easy and clear style.

WHERE DO I START?

You probably wouldn't want to start reading your way from one wall of a library to the other, and the same goes for the Bible. I have known people who have started off at the book of Genesis, but got bogged down somewhere in Leviticus, and gave up for years, before they found someone to suggest a better route.

One way of reading your Bible is to follow a study guide which will suggest a passage for each day and provide you with help in understanding it. You might work your way through one of the gospels, then go on to learn about an Old Testament prophet, and then look at one of Paul's or Peter's letters. These study guides are available from such people as Bible Reading Fellowship.

Another way of reading your Bible is to get a Bible study guide and then read at your own speed following a recommended route. This has the advantage of being flexible, and if you wanted you could read whole chunks of story sometimes, and go slowly, paragraph by paragraph, at others.

Here are some Bible study guides I would recommend:

The Lion Concise Bible Handbook

What the Bible Is All About (Mears Regal Books)

NIV Bible Commentary (Alister McGrath, Hodder and Stoughton)

Hayford's Bible Handbook (Jack W. Hayford, Nelson)

Or you can use the *NIV One Minute Youth Bible* (Hodder and Stoughton) which gives you short daily readings, study guide and commentary all in one.

Here, too, is one possible route for you to start with. You don't have to read each chunk at one sitting, of course. Take your time and enjoy it.

Title of book	What I learnt
2 Timothy 1:3-14	
Luke	
Acts 1-5	

Genesis 6-9

Genesis 15

Genesis 37-46

Exodus 1-4

Exodus 12:1-11

Exodus 15:1-21

Exodus 19-20

John

This doesn't cover all the Bible, but enough to begin with. Read one or two psalms in between these books, and dip into Proverbs as you go along as well. There are lots of other stories in the Bible which you are likely to enjoy. You can read about Ruth, Esther and Jonah in their own books, David and Goliath in 1 Samuel 17, and Paul's shipwreck in Acts 27 and 28 (up to verse 11). If you find you are getting bogged down anywhere, skim read to a place that catches your attention again.

As you read the Bible regularly you will find you are getting a richer and clearer idea of what God is like and how he behaves. You'll find some stories in the Bible giving you fresh understanding about something which is happening in society, or in your family, or in your own life. You won't always agree with what you are reading; the Bible is about real people, and they don't behave perfectly at all. There are documented stories of cruelty, selfishness, greed and corruption as well as cases of courage, honesty and goodness.

Overall the Bible tells the human story, and God's loving plan to rescue us from everything that threatens to destroy us, either from inside or outside ourselves. That story is gradually unfolded through the lives and mistakes of scores of ordinary people, and in particular by the life of God on earth in the person of Jesus, with the Old Testament looking towards his coming and the New Testament recording what happened when he came to live a human life on earth.

You will be able to read the Bible every day of your life and still find truths that are new and exciting. And you can start straight away if you like!

LIVING GOD'S WAY

The basic two rules for living God's way are these:

1. Love God with all your heart and mind and strength
2. Love your neighbour as yourself.

This is the way Jesus summed up (see Matthew 22:23-33; Mark 12:28-34 and Luke 20:27-40) the whole of the Jewish Law and the ten commandments given through Moses to the people after God had led them from slavery in Egypt and while they were wandering in the desert on the way to the Promised Land. (See Deuteronomy 6:4-5 for the first rule; and Leviticus 19:18 for the second.)

They are very clever rules because they are simple enough for us to learn by heart (and we should do that, so we always have them available in our minds) and they are deep enough to apply to every situation we could ever meet. That means that we can always measure our thoughts, words and actions by these two simple rules, and if they are true to these guidelines they are probably the right way to behave.

Let's look at the first rule first. We are not advised or asked to love God – we are told to. That is rather like the scout or guide law; you don't have to become a scout or guide, but if you do, you promise to keep the rules. That's how it is with us as Christians. God didn't force us all to be his followers, we are always free to choose. But if we do choose to live his way, then this is what we have to do.

The fact that we are told to love God makes it obvious that it can't be the emotional love which relies on feelings. If we are loving God with our minds and strength as well as our hearts then the love will carry on whether we happen to be feeling a warm glow or not; whether the sermon is boring or not; whether we are well or not; whether anyone else is or not.

The fact that we are told to love God with our minds suggests that God likes us to think about our faith and not accept everything we read simply because it's in print. It suggests that when our faith is challenged by someone else's doubts God wants us to work through those things and think them out in his company, rather than retreating into the company of other believers and never venturing out.

There were some Christians in the sixteenth century who refused to believe that the earth could be round, and had people severely punished for suggesting such a thing, even though the evidence was staring them in the face. They were too frightened to love God with their minds as well as their hearts; perhaps they were afraid their picture of God wouldn't stand up to the idea of a round world.

We can smile at that now, but there will be plenty of occasions through your life when new research may throw up new knowledge about our universe and you may be tempted to leave your mind at the church door when you worship God in case he turns out to be no match for these ideas.

Well, you needn't ever worry about that.

God is perfectly able to cope with everything. You can go on loving him with all your mind as well as your heart and strength because he encompasses all truth already. Some of that truth we haven't discovered yet, but God has, because he thought of it in the first place.

There are many Christian scientists who marvel freshly at the wonder of God every time they discover some new fact about the physical world.

Loving God is put as the first commandment because it is of more importance than anything or anyone else in our lives. When we get that right, the rest will follow. So you will need to be watchful in case anything (even a good thing) starts to take over that central place in your life which belongs to God.

What about the second rule, about loving your neighbour as yourself? It grows naturally out of loving God, because the more you love God the more you will find you are able to love other people – even those you don't warm to immediately.

As before, the love is not confined to those you are attracted to, and it involves showing the caring love in loving care. That means actually doing something to help. It means helping when you don't necessarily gain anything from it, except to know that you are doing what God needs doing.

Jesus was right – all the other commandments to do with our neighbour (do not kill,
do not spread false rumours, do not crave
what belongs to someone else, do not steal
other people's partners, do not take what
doesn't belong to you, honour your father
and mother), all these are covered by the rule
to love others as we love ourselves. If you
love them, you don't wrong them or wish
them harm.

So although I have no idea where your
life is going to lead you, what temptations
you will find particularly difficult, or what
sorrows you will have to face, I can still
show you a route through your life that will
work and bring you safely to heaven. It is
the way, or route, of God himself, summar-
ised in these rules by Jesus, which are like a
compass to take with you and check your
direction. Many people find it helpful to
have a spiritual friend, or guide, to keep in
touch with regularly – say four times a year.
For some reason this isn't often suggested to
young people, which I think is a pity. If your
parish doesn't provide it, you could show
them this book and suggest they start.

It's rather like the prayer partner idea we
talked about earlier, but for this you really
need to have someone a bit older than you,
whom you respect and find you can talk to.

The person should be a faithful Christian, whose life shows they are a good friend of God's. Then you have someone you can contact whenever you want to talk something over, or whenever you're worried about anything.

This person may be your parish priest or curate, or your school chaplain, the parent of one of your friends, a godparent, one of your teachers or someone at church you know well. You will probably build a relationship which lasts a lifetime, and you will be as helpful to them as they are to you.

You will need regular feeding on your journey, not just with chips and pizzas, but with spiritual food as well. God has thought of that and made excellent provision for us. All our prayer will feed us, and every time we take part in the eucharist and receive communion we will be receiving God's living presence into our lives.

There are churches all over the world, and in all of them which are in communion with the Roman Catholic Church you can share in the eucharist and receive communion. So you can make a point of using this valuable resource regularly all through your life, and wherever you travel.

I'm Sorry!

This section of your handbook is rather like a mountain guidebook which gives you a map of the terrain ahead, and points out the treacherous areas and where the best views are, where you can find refreshments and accommodation, and what protective clothing is advisable.

It is extremely likely that you, along with everyone else, will find times in your life that are happy and positive, and other times when there is a lot of pain and heartache for one reason or another. There will be times in your Christian journey when you stick with God and manage together to get through some terrible experiences and grow from having them. There may be other times when you decide to go off on your own, get into serious trouble and have to struggle over dangerous rocks to get back to the path again.

It isn't an easy option to be a Christian. Perhaps it should carry a Health Warning: 'Following Christ can be dangerous!' Jesus made a point of warning his friends that they would be persecuted and insulted for following him, and through the centuries that has proved to be true.

As you read this there are many people imprisoned in filthy conditions simply because they are Christian. Others have lost their jobs, or their children cannot get places at university. Still others can only be Christians secretly because if they came out their lives would be in danger.

And for you, too, there will be times when others in your school will make fun of you and make you feel embarrassed to admit that you are a committed Christian and know that God is real and is alive. There will be discussion groups when you will wonder if you can be brave enough to speak out for what you know is right because you know it will be different from what most other people think, and they may well think you are crazy.

Jesus knew all this would happen. He isn't like a pompous General, watching at a safe distance as all the soldiers charge helplessly into the teeth of the enemy. Instead Jesus showed in his life that he was prepared to stick with the loving, truthful way even when it made him so unpopular that he was tortured and nailed to a cross, to die in the most sordid and cursed way available.

So if and when you find yourself facing conflict and persecution of any kind, whether it's from people in your family, people at school, or anyone else, because of what you believe, then take to heart some of the things Jesus said and did. They won't make the difficulties melt away overnight (after all, as I said on page 14, God may be able to use this situation for great good if you let him) but they will give you comfort and reassurance, and remind you that you aren't ever on your own.

WORDS TO COMFORT AND ENCOURAGE YOU

And know that I am with you always; yes, to the end of time.   *Matthew 28:20*

There is no need to be afraid, little flock, for it has pleased your Father to give you the kingdom. *Luke 12:32*

May the Lord never allow you to stumble!
No, he sleeps not nor slumbers,
his people's guard . . .
The Lord will guard you from evil,
he will guard your soul,
The Lord will guard your going
and coming . . . *Psalm 121*

The Lord is close to all who call him,
who call on him from their hearts.
Psalm 145

I am the Way, the Truth and the Life.
John 14:6

Yes, God loved the world so much
that he gave his only Son,
so that everyone who believes in him may
not be lost
but may have eternal life. *John 3:16*

For human beings this is impossible;
for God everything is possible.
Matthew 19:26

Glory to him whose power, working in us, can do infinitely more than we can ask or imagine; glory be to him from generation to

generation in the Church and in Christ Jesus
for ever.   *Ephesians 3:20*

DEALING WITH SIN

Sometimes you will have got into a mess
through no one's fault but your own. Perhaps
you let your anger get the better of you and
said some really hurtful things which have
damaged a friendship. Perhaps you are
making life very difficult for someone you
live with. Perhaps you know you have a big
problem with telling the truth, or with self-
control.

It is as if you have been walking too
near the edge of one of those narrow, eroded
cliff paths, and have fallen into the thorns
and mud below. Your first reaction at such
times may well be to blame everyone but
yourself, and justify your actions energeti-
cally. Then, with God's spirit dwelling in
you, you might recognise that sneaking suspicion that is whispering, 'you're at least
partly to blame'.

That first nudging of your conscience
needn't make you wallow helplessly in guilt
for the rest of your life, but it does have to
be faced – this unpleasant truth that you
have sinned and done what is wrong (or
failed to do what is right). It may well make

79

you feel very sad and miserable, as you realise how you have hurt God and hurt others by your actions or thoughts or words.

This sorrow hurts, and you can do one of two things with it. Either you can bury it away and try to forget it, or you can let it lead you to repentance and forgiveness. God always leaves the choice up to you, however old you get, because of that gift of free will which we thought about on page 15.

Suppose you decide to bury it. Every time you bury something away like this you will grow a little more callous, a little harder, a little less able to hear your conscience giving you nudges. You might think this would result in a more carefree life, but sadly the opposite is true. Buried sin festers away inside, and grows roots of resentment and suspicion. It doesn't free you, but it can eventually choke your growth.

Suppose you let the sadness lead you towards wanting things to be put right again between you and God, and between you and whoever you have hurt. This longing is called repentance, which really means turning right round, away from the sin towards God. That turning around when you feel ashamed is a bit like having a filling at the dentist – you put up with it even though you wouldn't rate it top of the enjoyment list, because you know it's necessary, and will free you from long-term pain.

As soon as you begin to make that turn, God is there immediately to help you as much as he can. This is what he was hoping and hoping you would be courageous enough to do, and he, and all heaven's angels, are really happy for you. As you name your sin to God and tell him how you want to be rid of it all and to put things right, he will be there, not excusing you and pretending you didn't do it, but agreeing with you that it is wrong, and yet forgiving you completely because he loves you.

In the Catholic Church, this aspect of our life with God is considered so important that it is a sacrament – the sacrament of reconciliation. There are four basic movements to this dialogue of repentance with God, through the ministry of the Church. First, we let God speak to us (through hearing a passage from the gospels or another part of scripture); we turn to God and admit our sinfulness; we hear the Church pronounce God's forgiveness; but last, and not least, as a sign that our repentance is genuine, we have to go and live out that forgiveness, trying not to fall into the same trap.

Having God forgive your sin is absolutely and completely wonderful. It's like a long hot bath after a week at camp; or sighting the youth hostel when you thought you were lost; or being offered a lift home by your neighbour when you've missed the last bus and it's pouring with rain.

I have known this experience often because I have got into some terrible messes in my life, and every time I have hated the turning round, and every time I have been made so happy by God's loving forgiveness that I've wondered why on earth I took so long to get round to asking God's forgiveness!

So my advice is to turn round just as quickly as you become aware of your sin, and then you can get on with living freely again and not being weighed down with guilt and confusion.

In his letter to the Ephesians Paul talks about our need to wear protection against the evil in life. He suggests we put on spiritual armour: breastplate of righteousness, helmet of salvation, sword of the Spirit, shoes of the gospel of peace, belt of truth, shield of faith, cloak of love. With this as our protection and with God's help, we will always be safe!

SPREADING THE GOOD NEWS

Whenever you have some good news it's natural to want to spread it around, and as you find out more about God and the brilliant way he works, you'll be wishing your non-Christian friends could know him as well. But how can you do it, without turning them off?

Well, it's probably changes in you that they'll notice first, rather than things you tell them, so you don't need to bombard them with religion when they haven't a clue what you're talking about. (I know I was badly put off for several years because of someone trying that approach with me.)

The first thing you can do is to pray regularly and longingly for your friends to get to know the true God. You may only have to do this for a week. It may take twenty years. However long it takes, keep doing it and *never give up on them* because our God never gives up.

You will find that from time to time opportunities come up for you to talk about God. Work at their pace, never overpowering them, but dealing honestly with the question they're concerned about, and never forcing them to make a commitment. (God doesn't, so why should you?)

Love them, looking out for their needs and being available. Enjoy them. Value them as they are. These are God's ways, and his ways are the best.

Here are some questions which often puzzle people, and may help you and your friends.

Who made God?

Nobody. As we're humans, living in time, we tend to think God must be like everything else and have a beginning and an end. Well, if he was anything else he would have. But the fact that he's God means that he finds impossible things quite natural. Just as it's natural for an oak leaf to die and drop off the tree, so it's natural for God to be for ever, with no beginning and no end.

What is God like?

No one in this life has ever seen God, so we don't know what he looks like. But you can tell quite a lot about someone without seeing them. From the universe we can tell that God, who makes and sustains it, must be imaginative, organised, highly intelligent, enjoying variety, paying attention to detail, affectionate, full of integrity, faithful, respecting people and creatures, gentle, powerful, hopeful, and wise.

From Jesus, who was walking about on our planet as a human, we are shown in human terms what God is like. And we find someone full of love and compassion, with a sense of humour, able to understand people deeply, prepared to go to any lengths (even death) out of love for people. We find him wanting to set people free from pain, guilt, bitterness and selfishness. We find him a loyal friend who is prepared to stand up for what is right and good however unpopular this makes him. We find someone huge crowds seek out because his company is so attractive and fulfilling.

How can Jesus still be alive?

Jesus was killed on the Friday. By Sunday morning something extraordinary had happened, which is completely impossible by human standards. Jesus had gone through death and out into new life, appearing on many occasions to a lot of different people. He could not have done this if he was only a human. Having come through death to life he will stay alive for ever. So that means he is alive now.

If God is good and powerful, why doesn't he do something to stop the evil in the world?

Good question. It would seem sensible, wouldn't it? What it would mean, though, is that we would all be robots, programmed to do nothing but good. God wants something better for us than that. It's very risky, but he has created us with the power to choose good or evil in everything. It's rather like giving someone a sharp penknife – it works really well when you use it properly, but can go horribly wrong if you use it in a temper.

God has decided that we are worth the risk. He wants us to be free, and he hopes we will choose wisely. But he also knows there will be times when evil builds up as a result of wrong choices, and that's why he works so hard at using (or redeeming) evil for good.

What about natural disasters?

Our universe wasn't just made and dumped. It's being developed all the time. Our earth is still cooling, the skin of the planet is still flexible and on the move, the universe is still expanding. There's a lot of power in all this and sometimes people are bound to be involved when some of the power is released.

That doesn't mean that God shrugs his shoulders and isn't concerned. All his physical laws are vital for the universe to continue, but it grieves God deeply that even a sparrow should have to die. God shares with us the pain and tragedy of natural disasters, and does all he can to comfort, and bring some good from what is so heartbreaking.

Why did God create the world?

Because he wanted to. All of creation, including you, is the result of God's good idea.

<u>WHAT, ME?</u>

God has called you to be his follower and friend, and you have replied to his invitation and agreed to go with him. He will be able to work with you for the good of the world in all kinds of varied and exciting ways. He will never ask more of you than he knows you are able to cope with, and if ever he needs you to do a particular job he will always provide the resources and training you need.

You will find he has a way of using all your experiences (even the bad ones) at some point in your life, so nothing is ever wasted. He can use your failures as well as your successes.

I thought it might be an idea to list for you some of the jobs that are available for young Catholics, so that if you feel God is nudging you towards one you will know who to contact.

Ministry	Contact
AT CHURCH	
Eucharistic minister	Clergy
Choir member, member of music group.	Organist or clergy
Server	Clergy
Helping with children's ministry	Children's leader or clergy
Reader	Clergy
Member of parish council	Secretary
AT SCHOOL	
Assisting in chaplaincy work	Chaplain
Justice and peace group	Secretary
Writing for school magazine	Editor

Raising funds and awareness for charity

CAFOD
Romero Close, Stockwell Road
London SW9 9TY
Telephone: 020 7733 7900

Action Aid
Chataway House, Leach Road
Chard, Somerset TA20 1FR
Telephone: 01460 238000

Christian Aid
PO Box 100, London SE1 7RT

Many parishes have active Justice and Peace groups. Contact the local Secretary for details of activities.

Other organisations

Catholic Youth Services
39 Eccleston Square, London SW1V 1BX
Telephone: 020 7834 1175

Handicapped Children's Pilgrimage Trust
100a High Street, Banstead
Surrey SM7 2RB
Telephone: 01737 353311

IMPACT!
St Joseph's, Watford Way, London NW4 4TY
Telephone: 020 8203 6290

Young Christian Workers
St Joseph's, Watford Way, London NW4 4TY
Telephone: 020 8203 6290

Some Catholic organisations also have junior
sections, such as:

The Vincent de Paul Society
Damascus House, The Ridgeway,
London NW7 1EL
Telephone: 020 8906 1339

So you see, you don't have to go it alone! Even if there aren't many people of your age at your church there are millions of you around all over the world who are excited about God, and can't wait to start working and living to transform this world. May God bless you richly as you travel, and keep you safe in body and spirit. I will be praying for you, and perhaps, you can sometimes pray for me. Stick close to the God who loves you, and enjoy yourself!